GLOBAL WARMING, GREENHOUSE GASES AND RELATED FACTORS

WILLIAM PETRUK

FORWARD

Throughout its long history (4.6 billion years) earth has experienced many climate changes due to natural causes. Recently, the severity and frequency of hurricane's, floods, droughts and forest fires have increased, and glaciers are melting faster than usual. Many persons consider that the current climate changes are due to global warming caused by human-activities, especially activities that add greenhouse gases to the atmosphere. Other persons are skeptical.

Fortunately, a considerable amount of scientific research has been done on global warming, global cooling and greenhouse gases by environmentalists, climatologists, paleoclimatologists, geochemists, geologists, geophysicists, planetary scientists, and meteorologists at Government Agencies, NASA, Universities, Smithsonian National Museum of National History and others. The internet has incorporated the highlights of most research results in Wikipedia, NASA reports, MIT reports, University reports and others. Furthermore, industry has been adapt at implementing many of the research results.

This paper compiles and summarizes the highlights from internet reports and data on scientific research that directly and indirectly affects global warming and greenhouse gases during the current period as well as in ancient times.

**William Petruk, B.Eng., M.Sc., Ph.D. Earth Sciences,
Retired Research Scientist.**

Contents

ABSTRACT

This paper integrates the factors that are reported in scientific literature about global warming by greenhouse gases and about global temperatures on planet earth since it was created 4.6 billion years ago. According to the scientific reports, the terrestrial and ocean surfaces are warmed by infrared radiation of solar energy. The earth's atmosphere is warmed by infrared radiation from the terrestrial and ocean surfaces, as well as from solar energy, and by the action of greenhouse gases, especially carbon dioxide and methane (natural gas). There is a general correlation between the average earth's atmospheric temperature and the atmospheric carbon dioxide content.

The current concept of global warming is, "A rapid increase in earth's surface temperature". Scientific reports show that rapid increases in earth's surface temperature and of atmospheric carbon dioxide began in about 1980, hence we are experiencing global warming. It is generally accepted that, when global warming occurs, climate changes such as extreme storms, flooding, hurricanes, extreme blizzards, increased glacial melting, forest fires and drought tend to happen.

On the other hand, a certain amount of carbon dioxide is essential for life to exist on earth. Photosynthesis on plants, algae, bacteria, etc. converts the carbon dioxide in the atmosphere and oceans into carbohydrates as food for all organisms (plants, animals, bacteria, etc.) and oxygen (for
respiration). The process uses sunlight's energy, carbon dioxide and water. So life cannot exist without a certain amount of atmospheric carbon dioxide.

Throughout it's long history, earth has experienced long periods of extremely high carbon dioxide contents and high average temperatures, largely due to extreme ancient volcanism and outgassing of carbon dioxide.

Earth has also experienced five major ice ages during the last 2.4 billion years, and they had an impact on global warming. The greatest ice age lasted about 220 million years, from about 770mya to 550mya. It intermittently covered the entire planet with ice and snow, and is referred to as "Snowball Earth". That ice age ended with extreme volcanism and outgassing which produced an atmosphere with several percent carbon dioxide and extremely high temperatures.

We are currently in a warming interglacial period of the Quaternary sub-ice age that began about 2.58 million years ago. This sub-ice age had many glaciation cycles about every 100,000 years. Each glaciation cycle consisted of a glacial and an interglacial period that lasted at least 10,000 years (generally much longer). Some of the glacial periods during this sub-ice age were as cold as the ones during "Snowball Earth".

The highest atmospheric carbon dioxide content reached during the seven previous interglacial periods of this ice age was 300 ppm, but the atmospheric carbon dioxide content in the current interglacial period has already reached 417 ppm and could go higher. The temperature has increased about 1°C above the value that was reached in 1980. Since we are currently experiencing global warming due to greenhouse gases produced by human activities we do not know how warm the atmosphere will get.

PART 1

GLOBAL WARMING, GREENHOSE GASES AND HISTORIC TEMPERATURES

GLOBAL WARMING

The sun heats the earth through the radiation of infrared light. Roughly 30 % of the incoming sunlight (solar energy) is reflected into space by bright surfaces like clouds and ice. The remaining 70 % is absorbed by the land, oceans and atmosphere. The land and oceans emit the absorbed infrared thermal radiation into the atmosphere and back into space but at longer wavelengths. The atmosphere contains the greenhouse gases (in order of abundance); water vapor (H_2O), carbon dioxide (CO_2), methane (CH_4), nitrous oxide (N_2O), ozone (O_3) and trace amounts of chlorofluorocarbons (CFCs), and the non-greenhouses gases (in order of abundance); nitrogen (N), oxygen (O), argon (Ar) and trace amounts of other elements (Table 1).

Table 1
Composition of earth's atmosphere

Nitrogen (N)	78.08 %	
Oxygen (O)	20.95 %	
Argon (Ar)	0.93 %	
Carbon dioxide (CO_2)	0.0416 %	Greenhouse gas
Neon (Ne)	0.00182 %	
Methane (CH4)	0.000187 %	Greenhouse gas
Helium (He)	0.00052 %	
Krypton (Kr)	0.00011 %	
Hydrogen (H)	0.00005 %	
Xenon (Xe)	0.0000087 %	
Ozone (O_3)	0.000007 %	Greenhouse gas
Nitrous oxide (NO_2)	0.000002 %	Greenhouse gas
Water vapor	usually 1 to 3% (up to 5%)	Greenhouse gas

Greenhouse gases are defined as gases that absorb and emit radiant energy within the thermal infrared range. Hence, whenever they absorb energy, they will emit it, thereby producing the greenhouse effect and warming the atmosphere. The non-greenhouse gases do not absorb nor emit infrared energy. If there was no greenhouse effect, the average earth's atmospheric temperature would be about -18 °C, but with today's greenhouse effect, it is about 15 °C.

When the land and oceans are warmed by the sun, they radiate heat energy (thermal infrared radiation). This radiant energy warms the atmosphere and passes into space without being affected by non-greenhouse gases. On the other hand, greenhouse gas molecules, especially carbon dioxide, absorb and trap some of the heat energy (photons) that would otherwise go into space (Kroll, M.I.T). The photons are particles representing a quantum of light that carries energy but zero rest mass. This causes the bonds between the atoms of the greenhouse gases to vibrate, bend and stretch, and add additional heat to the atmosphere. Notably, the greenhouse gas molecules absorb infrared light at only specific conditions. For example, carbon dioxide molecules absorb photons at wavelengths around 15 microns, which are longer than the wavelengths that were disregarded in the incoming sunlight. Eventually, the greenhouse gas molecules release the photons; some go into space and some rebound into the atmosphere.

Global warming is defined as a "rapid increase in earth's surface temperature." A report by NASA for the period from "The beginning of the industrial age to the present date (1750 to 2020)" shows that the earth's surface temperature, carbon dioxide and methane rose rapidly during

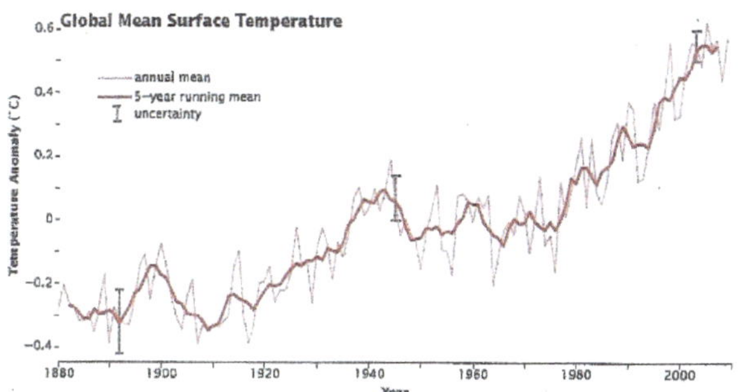

Despite ups and downs from year to year, global average surface temperature is rising. By the beginning of the 21st century, Earth's temperature was roughly 0.5 degrees Celsius above the long-term (1951–1980) average. (NASA figure adapted from Goddard Institute for Space Studies Surface Temperature Analysis.)

the period from 1980 to 2020 and confirms global warming since about 1980 (Figure 1).

Figure 1: (Reproduced from NASA, Earth Observatory report, Global Warming, June 3, 2010.

The correlation between atmospheric temperature

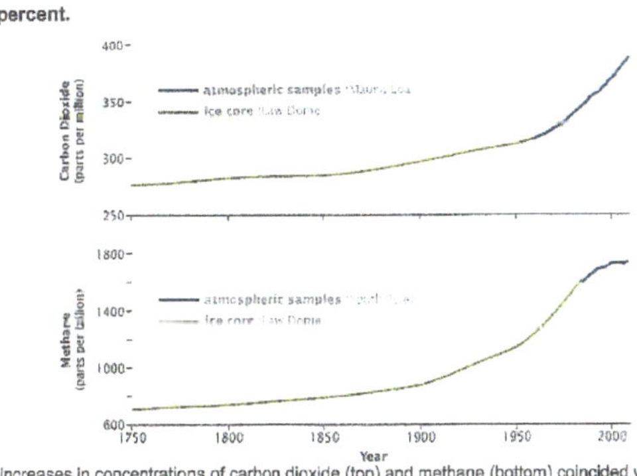

Increases in concentrations of carbon dioxide (top) and methane (bottom) coincided with the start of the Industrial Revolution in about 1750. Measurements from Antarctic ice cores (green lines) combined with direct atmospheric measurements (blue lines) show the increase of both gases over time. (NASA graphs by Robert Simmon, based on data from the NOAA Paleoclimatology and Earth System Research Laboratory.)

and carbon dioxide was further confirmed by two studies that involved drilling into Antarctic Quaternary glaciers which began 2.58 million years ago and covered the Antarctic and most of the northern hemisphere north of the 45 latitude with ice and snow. About 10 % of the Quaternary glacier still exists in the Antarctic, Greenland and mountain tops. The Quaternary ice age is continuing.

One Ice Core Project, The Vostock Ice Core Project, obtained ice core from surface to 400,000 years old ice (Figure. 2a), the other one, The EPICA Ice Core Project, obtained ice cores from surface to 800,000 years old ice (Figure 2b). The ice cores were analyzed using established techniques to determine the atmospheric temperatures and carbon dioxide contents during ice formation.

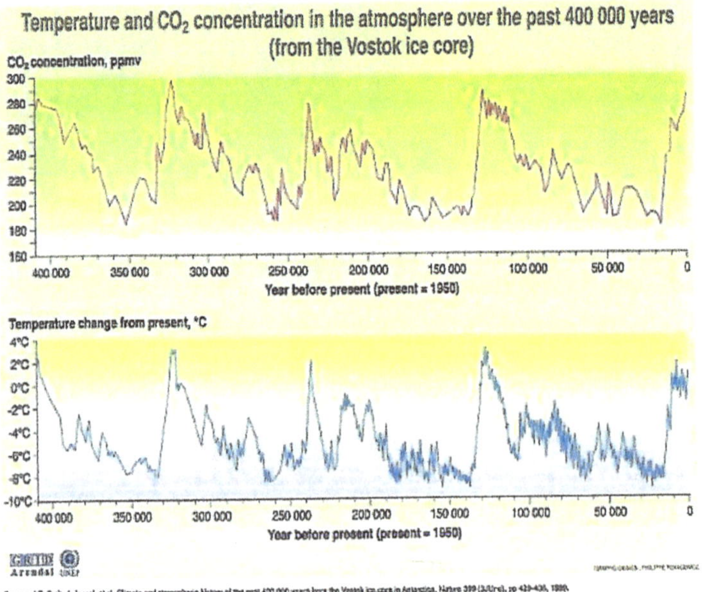

Figure 2a: Vostock ice core project. (Reproduced from NOAA report, communicating Science Programs)

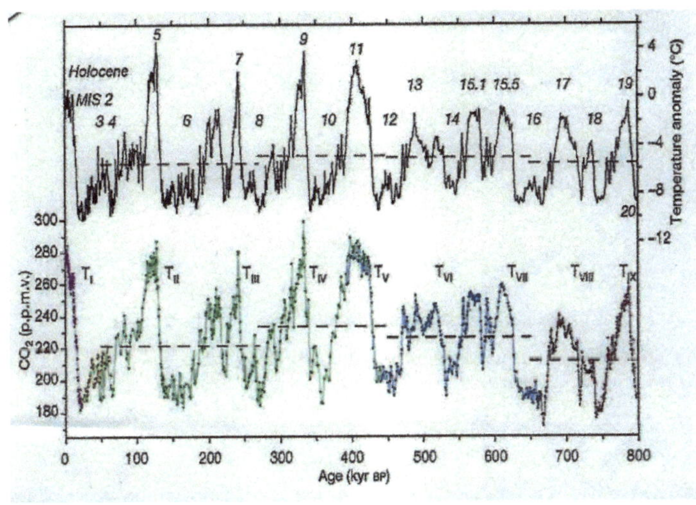

Figure 2b: EPICA ice core project. (Reproduced from NOAA report, communicating Science Programs) (Note that the decreasing age, as drawn in Figure 2a, is from left to right, whereas, in Figure 2b, the decreasing age is from right to left.)

The Vostock data shows that there were four glaciations in 400,000 years, and the EPICA data shows eight glaciations in 800,000 years. Each glaciation lasted about 100,000 years and consisted of a glacial and an interglacial period. We are in the latest interglacial period of the Quaternary ice age. The previous interglacial period lasted about 28,000 years. The last glacial period began about 26,000 years ago and produced ice sheets that were between 3 and 4 km. thick. The sea level had dropped to about 120 meters lower than the present. Melting of the last glaciers began about 15,000 years ago, and the current interglacial period began about 12,000 years ago. By about 6,000 years ago, the ocean surfaces had returned to near the current levels.

The causes of ice ages and the glacial-interglacial periods are not fully understood. Evidence suggests that cyclical changes in solar output, volcanism, changes in the earth's orbit, and other factors might be in action.

On the other hand, carbon dioxide (CO_2) levels have consistently been low during ice ages and glacial periods and high during interglacial periods and post-ice ages. It is not known whether the CO_2 levels are the causes or effects of the ice ages. Human activity began augmenting the carbon dioxide, methane and other trace greenhouse gases in the atmosphere at the beginning of the industrial age, about 1750 AD or earlier, and global warming was confirmed in about 1980. Since then, the frequency and severity of local storms, forest fires, and droughts have increased.

Based on orbital models, the current interglacial period will continue for another 23,000 years, but many factors, including human contributions, could extend the next glacial maximum to 50,000 or even 100,000 years from now.

Carbon dioxide is an extremely important gas in the atmosphere and oceans because:

(1)   it is essential for the existence of life on the planet, and

(2)   as a greenhouse gas, it adds additional heat to the atmosphere and produces global warming.

A simplified explanation regarding the existence of life on the planet relates to carbon dioxide being the main ingredient for photosynthesis.

Photosynthesis is a process that is stimulated by the energy of sunlight on live growth (plants, trees, algae, cyanobacteria, etc.) on both lands and in the photic zones of the oceans (0 to about 200 meters deep). The process uses sunlight, water and carbon dioxide (CO_2) in the atmosphere and oceans. It converts the carbon of carbon dioxide into carbohydrates (biomass) in plants, trees, algae, bacteria etc., as food for the existence and growth of all aerobic (oxygen-breathing) organisms (plants, animals, bacteria, cyanobacteria, algae, etc.) on earth. It also releases the oxygen from the carbon dioxide as free oxygen, which provides the organisms with essential energy for respiration and strength. The following chemical formula describes the photosynthesis process.

$$6\ CO_2 + 6\ H_2O + photons = C6H_{12}O_6 + 6O_2$$

or simply

carbon dioxide + water +sunlight = glucose (biomass) +oxygen

Since about 71.5 % of the earth's surface is oceans, about 70 % of the CO_2 on earth is dissolved in oceans. The terrestrial atmosphere contains only about 30 % of the earth's CO_2.

Nature has effectively coped with the excess carbon dioxide in the atmosphere and oceans during the Phanerozoic Eon (541 million years ago to the present date) by:

(1) Storing unused carbon biomass in sedimentary rocks. During metamorphism, the biomass (carbon) was converted into graphite and hydrocarbons (coal, oil, natural gas (methane)), which are commonly referred to as fossil fuels. The hydrocarbons remained in the earth's crust until humans began using them to heat their buildings, power their vehicles and equipment, and electrify their world. Without realizing it, they reconverted the stored carbon to carbon dioxide (CO_2) and released it into the atmosphere.

(2) Precipitating the dissolved carbon, calcium and cyanobacteria in the oceans as carbonate deposits (limestone ($CaCO_3$)), especially during the Cambrian, Ordovician and Silurian geologic periods. Unfortunately, humans began using limestone and releasing CO_2 into the atmosphere.

GREENHOUSE GASES

As stated above, greenhouse gases are gases that exist in the atmosphere and oceans and absorb and emit photons of energy. In order of abundance, they are; water vapor (H_2O), carbon dioxide (CO_2), methane (CH_4), nitrous oxide (N_2O), ozone (O_3) and trace amounts of chlorofluorocarbons (CFCs); water vapor accounts for the highest percentage of the greenhouse gases: between 36 % and 66 % for clear sky conditions, and 66 % to 85 % for cloudy days, but its greenhouse effect is limited because the average atmospheric lifetime of water molecules in the atmosphere is only nine days. On the other hand, carbon dioxide (CO_2), which accounts for only about 9 to 26 % (rarely to 39 %) of greenhouse gases, is a significant greenhouse gas because its average atmospheric lifetime can last from a few years to over a   century. Thus, carbon dioxide (CO_2) is the key reason for global warming. Methane (natural gas) accounts for about 4 to 9 % of greenhouse gas; its average atmospheric lifetime is around 12 years. It is noteworthy that, for the same mass, the greenhouse effect of methane (CH_4) is much greater than that of carbon dioxide (8 to 84 times greater, nominally 30 times greater) because methane contains hydrogen that produces a complex chemical reaction as a greenhouse gas. However, the earth's atmosphere contains much less methane than carbon dioxide (CO_2), so the effect of methane is much smaller than that of carbon dioxide.

Carbon Dioxide

As stated above, carbon dioxide is a fundamental ingredient for photosynthesis which is a process that produces the essentials of life for all aerobic organisms (bacteria, plants, animals, etc.) on earth. It is also a greenhouse gas that warms the earth for comfort. Too much CO_2 in the atmosphere and oceans causes global warming and acidifies the oceans, killing some ocean creatures. Some carbon dioxide is produced and removed by natural processes. Recently, the production and removal of carbon dioxide have been augmented by human activities.

Production of Carbon Dioxide by Natural Processes

(1) Animals and aerobic organisms exhale carbon dioxide when they consume and oxidize carbohydrates. The human body produces about 1 kg of carbon dioxide per day.

(2) Carbon dioxide is released when aerobic organisms decompose into organic material.

(3) Some carbon dioxide escapes from soils into the atmosphere.

(4) Carbon dioxide is released from the earth's crust by volcanoes, geysers and hot springs.

(5) Carbon dioxide is produced when limestone is dissolved in weakly acidic water (H_2CO_3). For example, the dissolution of limestone rocks in caves.

(6) Forest fires produce large amounts of carbon dioxide. The cause of forest fires is debatable, lightning, human carelessness, industrial activities?

(7) Coal-seam fires.

Uncontrolled coal seam fires are the most persistent fires on earth and can burn for thousands of years. Thousands of coal seams are burning at any given moment throughout the world and continue to burn as long as oxygen and coal are available. Most coal seam fires exhibit smoldering combustion because of limited atmospheric oxygen, but they keep burning until either the fuel(coal) is exhausted or an oxygen barrier is installed. It is estimated that the oldest known coal fire, the Burning Mountain in Australia has burned for 6,000 years.

Coal seam fires are ignited in many ways. Many are self-ignited if fine coal dust is exposed to the air. Forest fires, lightning, accidents and practices that produce a spark near coal seams will start coal-seam fires. The fires release toxic gases such as carbon monoxide (due to incomplete carbon combustion), sulfur, and mercury. The coal seam fires release about 3 % of the world's carbon dioxide emissions into the atmosphere. The major coal seam fires are in China, Indonesia, Germany, the United States, and India, and smaller ones are in Canada, New Zealand, South Africa and Norway.

Production of Carbon dioxide by Human Activities

(1) The combustion of carbon-based fuels (gasoline, diesel, kerosene, propane, natural gas (methane), coal, wood, and generic organic matter (biological fuels)) for heating, generating electricity, transportation, manufacturing, farming, etc.

(2) Thermal decomposition of limestone ($CaCO_3$) to manufacture quicklime and cement.

(3) Smelting oxide ores with metallurgical coal removes oxygen from the metals in the ore and produces carbon dioxide.

(4) Carbon dioxide is a by-product of fermentation in brewing alcoholic and other beverages.

(5) Deforestation, especially in the Amazon region and underdeveloped countries.

(6) Forest fires. The cause of forest fires is debatable. The unofficial estimate is that the emissions from the 2017 forest fires in BC were two to three times the emissions from fossil fuel burning from all other sectors in BC that year (Pacific Institute for Climate solutions). The emission of CO_2 from the 2021 forest fire in BC was probably greater than in 2017. Forest fires in 1997 in Indonesia were estimated to have

released 0.81 to 2.57 gigatonnes of CO_2, which is about 13 % - 40 % of the annual global carbon dioxide emissions from burning fossil fuels that year. (See section on forest fires).

Removal of carbon Dioxide by Natural Processes

(1) Photosynthesis on land, in oceans, mangroves, wetlands, and in lakes and rivers converts the CO_2 to carbohydrates and biomass. The carbohydrates and biomass are partly consumed by live organisms (bacteria, plants, animals, etc.). The remainders sink into oceans and, along with the remains of dead organisms, are incorporated into sedimentary rocks. Eventually, they become hydrocarbons (fossil fuels).

(2) Carbon dissolves in oceans and fresh waters. Some of the dissolved carbon in oceans precipitates as $CaCO_3$, with and without cyanobacteria, and eventually becomes limestone formations.

(3) Absorption of carbon dioxide into soils.

Human Activities that could Remove Carbon Dioxide

(1) Replace internal combustion engines with electric motors (electric cars, etc.). (Manufacturing cars produces carbon dioxide)

(2) use natural gas instead of coal for generating electricity, as natural gas emits 44 % less CO_2 than coal to release the same amount of energy.

(3) Capturing CO_2 and storing it in geological formations (debatable).

(4) Generate electricity by nuclear. (Building nuclear facilities produces carbon dioxide)

(5) Solar panels and windmills generate electricity. (Manufacturing solar panels and windmills produces carbon dioxide)

(6)   Using carbon dioxide in the Food industry, Oil industry, Chemical industry and others.

- Production of methanol and a range of other products
- propellant and acidity regulators in the food industry.
- Production of carbonated soft drinks, beer, sparkling wine, etc.
- Compressed gases for a variety of uses.
- fire extinguisher
- many other applications

It is considered noteworthy that about 550 million years ago (mya), there was a colossal outgassing of carbon dioxide that increased the CO_2 concentration in the atmosphere and oceans to enormous levels. That outgassing event followed an extremely severe ice age that lasted intermittently for 220 million years, from about 770 to 550 mya. At times the glaciation extended across the equator, and the entire planet was covered with ice and snow. Scientists refer to it as "Snowball Earth."

The outgassing caused extreme greenhouse conditions and prominent carbonate deposition as limestone formations. Consequently, most of the sedimentary rocks that were deposited during the Cambrian, Ordovician and Silurian periods (541 to 419 mya) were limestone formations; in particular, most of the rocks in the Niagara Escarpment are limestone of the late Ordovician and early Silurian periods. Since then, the carbon dioxide content in the atmosphere has decreased slowly. By the Jurassic period (201 to 145 mya), the carbon dioxide content was still 4 to 5 times greater than today. The current content of CO_2 in the atmosphere is about 0.0416 % (416 ppm); at the beginning of the industrial period (about 1750 AD), it was about 0.028 % (280 ppm).

It is noteworthy that the most remarkable development, creation and growth of animals and plants on earth occurred during the period of

541 to 49 mya when the carbon dioxide content was greater than at least four times its current level, and the average temperatures were around 30°C. However, from about 360 mya to 260 mya, there was an ice age with interglacial periods. During that time (The carboniferous period (359 to 299 mya), the oxygen levels in the atmosphere fluctuated between 15 % and 30 % and reached 35 %. The high oxygen levels may have contributed to the large size of insects and amphibians. The current oxygen level in the atmosphere is 20.95 %.

Methane (Natural gas)

Methane (CH_4), which is commercially referred to as natural gas is another greenhouse gas that has a major impact on global warming, but it behaves differently than other fossil fuels because it contains hydrogen. Scientific studies have shown that, for the same mass, the greenhouse effect of methane varies from 84 to 8 times greater than the greenhouse effect of carbon dioxide, nominally 30 times greater. I calculated that 72. 5 % of the greenhouse effect in the current atmosphere is due to carbon dioxide and 27.5 % to methane. I did the calculation by using the CO_2 and CH_4 contents in the atmosphere (Table 1), the greenhouse factor of 30 times greater for CH_4 than for CO_2, and disregarded other greenhouse gases.

The current methane content in the atmosphere (1866 ppb) has increased 156 % since about 1750 AD. For comparison, the percentage increase of other greenhouse gases is about 47 % for carbon dioxide and 23 % for nitrous oxide. The escalation of methane content could be due to the production of methane in the subsea floor by anaerobic methanogens that produce methane (see Oceans, page 38).

In contrast, the combustion of methane (CH_4) produces more energy per mass than the combustion of any other hydrocarbon because the mass of a methane molecule (CH_4) is lighter than the mass of a hydrocarbon molecule (C_2). Hydrogen has an atomic weight of 1, whereas carbon has an atomic weight of 12. Furthermore, the combustion products of methane are only water vapor plus 44 % less CO_2 than the combustion of coal or 29 % less CO_2 than the combustion of gasoline. This occurs because: upon combustion, methane's hydrogen produces 55% of the heat of combustion and creates only water (H_2O), whereas the methane's carbon adds 45 % to the heat of combustion and creates CO_2. This dream hydrocarbon gas, which produces only water and less CO_2 per mass than other hydrocarbons, has become a major fuel for:

- home and industrial heating,
- replacing coal for generating electricity,
- transitioning from diesel and gasoline into liquid natural gas (LNG) as fuel (BC ferries),
- many other applications.

In summary:

(1)   Upon combustion, methane becomes a dream gas because it produces more energy per mass than any other fossil fuel and releases only water and a reduced amount of carbon dioxide into the atmosphere.

(2)   Uncombusted methane released into the atmosphere, is the worst possible greenhouse gas.

On the other hand, some uncombusted natural gas

Worldwide methane leaks;
Blue lines = pipelines: orange dots = methane emissions.
@ Kayrros Inc. Garmin, FAO, NOAA, USGS, Open Street Map
contributors, and GIS User Community.

(methane) was either intentionally released or

Fig. 3: Worldwide Losses of Methane (Natural gas)
accidently leaked from wells, pipelines and production
facilities, and thus is a greenhouse gas. A research team under
Thomas Lauvaux at the Laboratory for Sciences of Climate
and Environment near Paris studied satellite images through
an algorithm that automatically detected plumes of methane
streaming into the atmosphere from oil and gas facilities
worldwide from 2019 through 2020 (Fig. 3). The view
revealed 1,800 methane plumes from gas operations and
pipelines; 1,200 were primarily in western Asia and USA. The
methane plumes were emitting about 10 % to 12 % of the
total emitted methane on earth. Ultra-emitters were pumping
more than 25 tonnes of methane per hour. Turkmenistan was

the biggest ultra-emitter, emitting more than a million tonnes of methane between 2019 and 2020. Russia was second at just under a million tonnes, followed by the U.S.A., Iran, Algeria, and Kazakhstan. The Chinese gas deposits and the USA shale gas deposits in mid-west USA could not be included in the survey because the methane above those deposits and facilities was like a cloud rather than a plume. According to Statistics Canada, one of the world's largest and longest natural gas pipeline networks is in Canada. The survey of pipeline leaks did not detect many leaks from the Canadian network (see Fig. 3).

The countries that contain the major methane (natural gas) deposits, in order of abundance, are Iran, Qatar, Russia, Turkmenistan, USA and Canada.

Occurrence of Methane

Methane occurs in natural gas fields, oil and gas fields, coal deposits, oil shales, wetlands, permafrost, on continental shelves in the Arctic and Antarctic oceans, and in ruminants (cattle, pigs, chickens, termites). The major natural gas deposits, in order of abundance, are Iran, Qatar, Russia, Turkmenistan, USA and Canada. Each type of occurrence of methane (natural gas) has specific characteristics and is referred to here as a specific category.

Natural gas fields

The Natural Gas fields occur as deposits in sedimentary strata. The largest known Natural Gas Field on earth is in the sedimentary strata under the Persian gulf and is shared by

Iran and Qatar. On the other hand, the natural gas

fields in the Yamburg and Urengoy regions in northwestern Russia are so large that they supply the European countries with 40 % of their natural gas needs via pipelines across Russia, Ukraine and throughout Europe. Other large natural gas fields are in Turkmenistan, and smaller ones occur in Kazakhstan and elsewhere.

One of the world's large natural gas fields, the Darvaza deposit in Turkmenistan, was purposely ignited in 1971 and it is still burning. The Darvaza crater covers an area of about 1 ½ acres and is about 60 feet deep. A large plume

Fig. 4: Darvaza gas crater

of fire is in the middle and smaller fires are burning throughout the crater. The crater is relatively unknown, but is a small tourist attraction referred to as Gates of Hell or "Door to Hell".

Natural gas in oil and gas fields

The natural gas deposits that occur in oil and gas fields range from those that contain small amounts of natural gas on top of oil deposits to those that consist mainly of natural gas with some oil. They occur in Middle Eastern countries and in the USA, Mexico, Central America, Canada and Alaska.

Natural gas in coal fields

Natural gas is present in all coal mines and is a hazard to coal miners. Some natural gas is recovered from coal mines, particularly in the eastern USA.

Natural gas in shales.

Considerable resources of methane occur as shale gas in sedimentary rocks, especially in USA and Canada. Shale gas requires artificially created fractures by hydraulic fracturing (fracking) to allow the gas to flow. The procedure involves drilling vertically to the natural gas bearing horizon, then pointing the drill to follow the horizon horizontally for hundreds or thousands of feet. Water mixed with a variety of chemicals is forced through the wellbore casing. The high-pressure water breaks up the rock and releases the natural gas (see Figure 10, page 25 in the Methane section).

Methane on continental selves in arctic and Antarctic oceans

Significant reservoirs of hydrate methane have been found in arctic and Antarctic permafrost and along continental margins beneath the ocean floor in the Polar Regions. The hydrate methane (clathrates) occurs as cages of water molecules that trap single molecules of methane. These deposits are a potential source of methane, but production would be complicated and expensive. A friend, Gerry MacMillan, described a PBS - TV program that showed small, isolated craters which were produced by natural explosions of local hydrate methane deposits in permafrost in northern Russia and Alaska.

Biogenic methane in ruminants and wetlands

Some of the earth's methane is biogenic and occupies landfills, soils, ruminants (cattle, chickens, pigs), guts of termites, and oxygen-depleted sediments below seafloors, lake bottoms, and rice fields. Some methane escapes into the atmosphere from soils and wetlands. Ruminants belch significant amounts of methane emissions to the atmosphere, accounting for about 22 % of the USA's emissions of methane to the atmosphere.

Processing Natural gas

Natural gas needs to be prepared for the consumer. It is processed to remove unwanted elements, compounds and solids, as well as acids that would corrode the pipelines that transport the gas to the consumer. Furthermore, a smell needs to be added to the gas so that its presence can be detected because natural gas is odorless and colorless. Liquid natural gas (LNG) is prepared at natural gas facilities for a variety of uses.

HISTORIC GLOBAL TEMPERATURES ON EARTH

Global temperatures from 2500 BC to 2040 AD.

On January 10, 2021, Randy Mann, a Meteorologist, published a picture on the internet about Global temperatures from 2500 BC to 2040 AD.

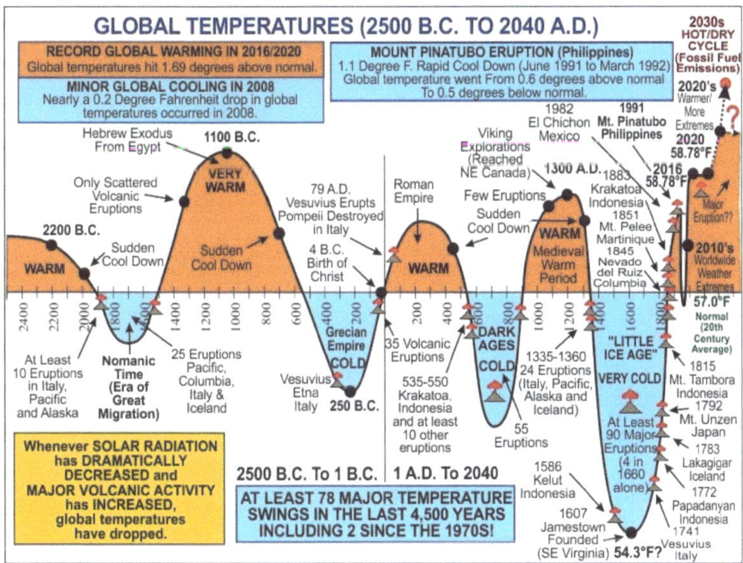

Figure 5: Reproduced from the report, Global Temperatures, by Meteorologist Randy Mann

Figure 5 shows:

- A warm period during the major Egyptian Dynasties (about +2500 BC to 575 BC.)
- The cold period during the Grecian, Phoenician, and Carthaginian Empires (575 BC to 0 AD.)
- Cold and Warm period during the Roman empire (about 200 BC to 535 AD.)
- The cold period during the Dark ages (535 AD to 900 AD.)

- Warm Medieval period (900 AD to 1350 AD.)
- Little Ice Age (1350 AD to 1850 AD), which was very cold in Europe.
- Warming period, early industrial age (1850 AD to 1980 AD.)
- Global warming (1980 AD to present).
- Numerous volcanic eruptions, including:
    (1) Mt. Tambora eruption in 1815, the largest recorded in human history, covered the earth with volcanic ash and dust for about a year, and there was essentially no summer in 1816;
    (2) Mt. Pinatubo eruption, June 1991 to March 1992, produced a temperature drop of 1.1 degrees.

66 million years of earth's history

On September 10, 2020, researchers at the University of California, Santa Cruz, California, published an article in SciTech Daily on the internet entitled "66 Million Years of Earth's Climate History Uncovered - Puts Current Changes in Context". They determined the global temperatures by accepted methods, which was measuring Oxygen isotope values in benthic foraminifera from sediment cores and reported the data as "Average Global Surface Temperature Difference with respect to 1961 - 1990 °C" (Figure 6). They classified temperature periods as Hothouse, warm house, Coolhouse and Icehouse

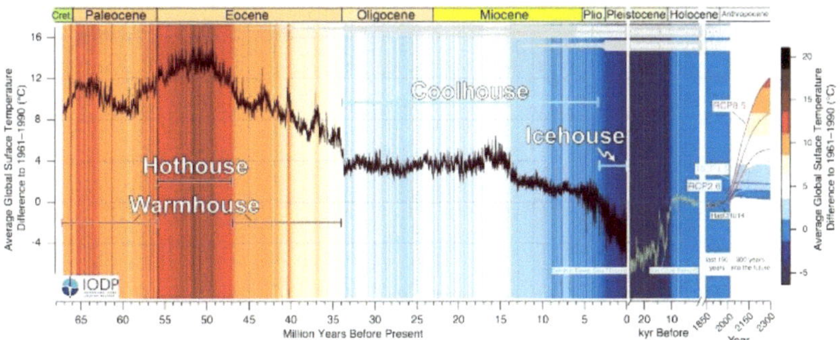

Figure 6 : (Reproduced from University of California report, "66 Million Years of Earth's Climate History Uncovered - Puts Current Changes in Context").

The researchers pointed out that rhythmic variations in temperature changes correspond to changes in the earth's orbit around the sun (variations due to the eccentricity of the earth's orbit and the precession and tilt of its rotational axis). They did not identify the specific temperature changes. *I interpret, from figure 6, that the changes in earth's orbit occurred at 34 million years (mya), 14 mya and 4 mya, i.e., at 10 and 20 million-year cycles.*

The figure also shows that from 66 to 4 million years ago (mya), the earth's temperature was continuously considerably higher than the temperature of the base period (1961 AD to 1990 AD). In particular, from 66 to 34 mya earth's temperature was 5 to 13 degrees higher than the base; from 34 to 15 mya, it was 4 to 5 degrees higher than the base, and from 14 to 4 mya, it steadily decreased from 4 degrees above the base temperature to the base temperature at 4 mya.

At 56 to 47 million years ago, there was a major increase in temperature to a peak of 13°C above the base, probably due to carbon dioxide, but it is uncertain where the carbon dioxide came from and what the sequence of events was. Scientists considered volcanic activities on the ocean floors but have not found volcanoes on the ocean floor. They also considered the release of methane from warming ocean sediments (see sections on methane and oceans) and the thawing of permafrost.

Temperatures on earth from 500 million years ago to present

The distribution of average global temperatures on earth from 500 million years ago to the present was compiled by a team of scientists at the Smithsonian National Museum of Natural History from data obtained by paleoclimatologists, paleontologists, climatologists, geochemists, geologists, planetary scientists, and others at universities, NASA, earth and planetary Institutes, National Climatic Data Centre, Smithsonian Museum of Natural History, and elsewhere (Figure 7). The diagram shows that throughout most of the Phanerozoic eon (541mya to present), the average earth's temperature was hotter than 68°F (20°C) (red), with cooler (blue) periods occurring only during the Ordovician ice age (450 mya to 420 mya), the Karoo ice age (360 mya to 260 mya, i.e., Carboniferous-Permian periods), and the Late Cenozoic ice age (34 mya to present). The current average

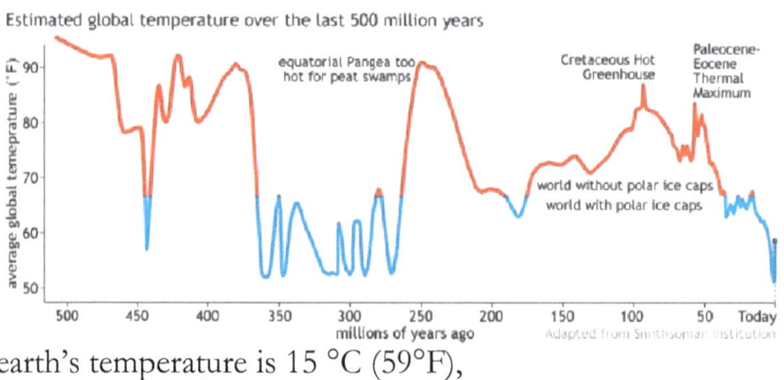

earth's temperature is 15 °C (59°F),

Figure 7: (Reproduced from, Reports, Smithsonian National Museum of Natural History)

We are currently in the latest interglacial period of the Quaternary sub-ice age, which is part of the Late Cenozoic ice age. The Quaternary sub-ice age began 2.58 mya and produced the coldest period on earth since the Snowball ice age (see the section on glaciers).

It has been shown above that carbon dioxide is a major factor in controlling the earth's atmospheric temperature. The outgassing of about 550 mya created a very high carbon dioxide content in the atmosphere and produced temperatures above 32°C (90°F). Those high temperatures continued for about 200 million years, regained after the Karoo ice age, then decreased to around 20 °C (68°F). Figure 5 shows that there was an addition of volcanic carbon dioxide at 90 mya and of oceanic methane and carbon dioxide at 56 mya (see page 19). Currently, human activities are contributing carbon dioxide to the atmosphere and producing global warming. Humans developed about less than 1 million years ago, and modern human civilization developed over just the past 11,000 years or so. My comment: this is the first time that human activities are contributing large amounts of carbon dioxide to the earth's atmosphere. There is no comparable experience for coping with such unwanted carbon dioxide in the atmosphere and Oceans.

PART 2

FACTORS THAT AFFECT GLOBAL WARMING

CARBON

Carbon is the main constituent of the greenhouse gases: carbon dioxide (CO_2) and methane (CH_4). It is element 6 of the periodic table with symbol C and atomic weight 12. Carbon is the fourth most abundant element in the universe after hydrogen, helium and oxygen. It is abundant in the sun, stars, comets, carbon-rich asteroids, and atmospheres of most planets in the solar system. The earth contains about 4,360 million gigatonnes of carbon at 730 ppm (2,000 ppm in the core and 120 ppm in the combined mantle and crust). Carbon is the 17th most abundant element in the earth's crust at 200 ppm. The atmosphere contains about 900 gigatonnes of carbon as CO_2 and methane (CH_4), and the oceans and lakes contain about 36,000 gigatonnes of carbon as dissolved carbon, CO_2 and methane (CH_4)

Carbon is essential for life and is a common element in all known life on earth. It is the second most abundant element in the human body (about 18.5 %) after oxygen.

Some properties of solid phases of carbon

- Melting point: carbon has no melting point. It remains solid at higher temperatures than the highest melting point of metals such as tungsten and rhenium. It sublimates at 700°C in an oxygen atmosphere to form carbon dioxide ($2O + C = CO_2$).

- Mohs hardness: graphite 1-2 (one of the softest minerals); diamond 10 (hardest mineral in earth's crust).
- Resists Reactions: at standard temperatures, carbon does not react with oxygen, sulfuric acid, hydrochloric acid, chlorine or alkalis but reacts with nitric acid.
- Reacts with oxygen at elevated temperatures: carbon robs oxygen from metals, as in iron smelting.
  ($2Fe_3O_4 + 4C = 6Fe + 4CO_2$)

Carbon in the earth's crust

Carbon occurs in the earth's crust as hydrocarbons (coal, oil, natural gas, methane), carbonate formations, graphite, allotropes of carbon (graphene, soot, charcoal, etc.), and diamonds. Regarding global warming, the hydrocarbons contain carbon dioxide and methane, and the carbonate formations (limestone) contain carbon dioxide.

Hydrocarbons

The hydrocarbons were produced as carbon biomass by photosynthesis on plants on land and in the oceans during the Paleozoic, Mesozoic and Cenozoic eras (541 million years ago to present) and earlier. Some of the biomass was eaten by animals, and they exhaled a small part back into the atmosphere as carbon dioxide. Dead plant material releases a small amount of carbon dioxide into the atmosphere while decaying. The remaining biomass and the decayed plant material became part of sedimentary rocks where, during the geological time, they were converted into hydrocarbons (coal, oil, natural gas (methane)) by metamorphism (heat and pressure).

It was estimated that photosynthesis converts about 100 to 115 billion tonnes of carbon per year and transfers it from the atmosphere into the biomass in the plants. When the hydrocarbons are used as fuel or heat, the reaction is reversed, and the carbon in the hydrocarbons is converted back to carbon dioxide in the atmosphere. It was estimated that human activities convert about 29 billion tonnes of carbon into carbon dioxide per year.

The quantities of carbon in hydrocarbons of the earth's crust have been estimated as follows:

- coal; known reserves, 900 gigatonnes, total coal, about 1,800 gigatonnes,
- oil; known reserves, about 150 gigatonnes, total, unknown. It was estimated that about 10 % of the oil was formed during the Paleozoic era (540 to 252 mya), 70 % during the Mesozoic era (252 to 66 mya) and 20 % during the Cenozoic era (since 66 million years ago).
- natural gas (methane); proven sources,105 gigatonnes, total, about 550 gigatonnes,
- shale gas (methane); estimated 540 gigatonnes,
- methane hydrates (clathrates): in polar regions under the sea (estimated 300 gt.).
- additional methane (CH_4); in soils, wetlands, and ruminants (cows, pigs, sheep).

Carbonate formations

Carbon is a principal constituent of the carbonate rock formations that account for about 20 to 25 % of the sedimentary rocks in the earth's crust. Most of the carbonate formations are composed of limestone, which consists of mineral calcite ($CaCO_3$) and contains minor amounts of clastic sediments (finely broken rock pieces). A few of the carbonate formations are composed of the mineral dolomite

((CaMg(CO$_3$)2) and are referred to as "dolomites." The carbon content of calcite is 12 % and of dolomite is 13 %.

Although limestones and dolomites are sedimentary rocks, they did not form in the same manner as other sedimentary rocks, which is by sedimentation of broken rock material. Instead, dissolved calcium and carbon dioxide in ocean waters was precipitated through biological and non-biological processes.

Numerous articles in Wikipedia reported the generally accepted theory that a gigantic volcanic outgassing episode occurred about 550 million years ago and raised the carbon dioxide concentration to inordinate levels in the atmosphere and oceans. It caused extreme greenhouse conditions in the atmosphere and carbonate deposition of limestone as the primary sedimentary rocks during the Cambrian, Ordovician and Silurian periods (541 to 419 million years ago).

Graphite

Graphite is composed of carbon and is widely used, but it does not impact global warming. It is a black metallic form of crystalline carbon that consists of layers of plate-like particles bonded together and occurs as flakes and masses as flaky intergrowths of carbon. Graphite occurs in metamorphic sedimentary rocks, as most of it formed by conversion of the carbon in hydrocarbon-bearing shales and limestone when the rocks were subjected to pressures of 75,000 pounds per square inch and temperatures in the range of 750 °C during intense regional metamorphism.

A small amount of graphite occurs in hydrothermal deposits (deposits from lava that cooled in the earth's crust).

The principal export sources of mined graphite are China, Mexico, Canada, the United States, Madagascar, India, Sri Lanka, Brazil, Turkey and North Korea.

Graphene

Individual plate-like layers in the graphite crystals are called graphene and are the strongest material ever tested. Further technological development is required before graphene can be economical for industrial processes.

Amorphous carbon

Other allotropes of carbon are amorphous carbon and are present as charcoal, lampblack, soot, and activated carbon.

Diamond

The mineral diamond occurs as clear and lightly colored cubic crystals that have very strong carbon-carbon bonds to form the hardest naturally occurring substance (Moh's hardness 10). It occurs in Kimberlite rocks in ancient volcanic pipes in South Africa, Namibia, Botswana, the Republic of Congo, Sierra Leone, India, arctic Russia, Canada, Brazil, Australia, USA, Zimbabwe, Angola and the ocean floor of Cape of Good Hope. Diamond ore is carefully crushed to prevent destroying larger diamond crystals. Then it is concentrated by density, assisted by X-ray fluorescence, as diamond is slightly heavier than rock minerals. Finally, it is recovered by hand sorting. Nine new diamond mines started production in the last ten years, most in Canada.

The diamond industry falls into two categories: gem-grade diamonds and industrial diamonds. About 80% of mined diamonds are unsuitable as gemstones and are used as industrial diamonds. Synthetic diamonds, invented in the 1950s, are widely used in industrial applications.

OCEANS

The oceans cover about 71 % of the earth's surface and account for about 97.5 % of the water on earth. They are estimated to represent about 0.023 % of the mass of the planet, and scientific studies show that water has been on earth since shortly after the planet's development. Multiple geochemical studies concluded that asteroids are the most likely primary source of earth's water.

Carbon dioxide dissolves in ocean waters. Some is removed from the oceans by photosynthesis which transfers the carbon to plants and marine organisms, and some is removed by precipitation as limestone. In this respect, the oceans, as well as coastal marine habitats such as mangroves and saltwater marshes, are enormous carbon dioxide sinks and have taken up a proportion of the CO_2 emitted by human activity. Furthermore, oceans influence climate and weather patterns.

Although the solubility of carbon dioxide in water is 28 times greater than the solubility of oxygen in water, the solubilities of both carbon dioxide and oxygen decrease with increasing temperatures in salt waters. At 5 °C, salt water contains about 7.2 ml/liter of oxygen, and at 25°C, it contains only about 4.95 ml/liter of oxygen. Increasing concentrations of carbon dioxide (CO_2) in the atmosphere leads to higher concentrations of CO_2 in ocean waters and produce ocean acidification (carbonic acid, H_2CO_3). Acidified oceans adversely impact marine organisms such as corals and crustaceans, whose structures are vulnerable in acid waters.

Ocean temperatures depend on the amount of solar radiation reaching the ocean surface. The temperatures of ocean surfaces range from around 30°C in the tropics to -2 °C. near the poles. Deep sea waters are between 5 °C. and -2

°C. Hence, much less atmospheric carbon dioxide dissolves in the oceans at the equator than at the poles (Figure 8).

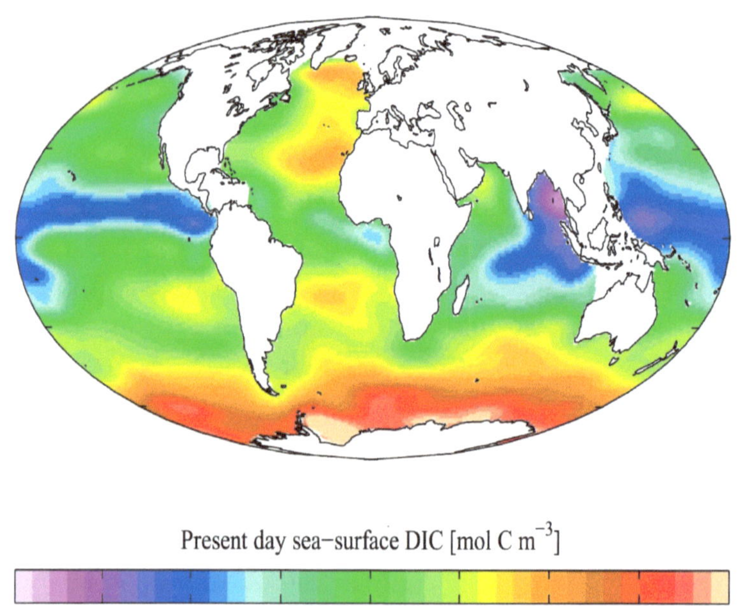

Figure 8: Distribution of dissolved organic carbon on ocean surfaces. (from Wikipedia "Carbon").

The density of seawater increases as the temperature decreases. Consequently, cold seawater is heavier than warm seawater and sinks deeper into the oceans. Passengers on cruise ships to the Antarctic observed strong demarcations where cold sea- waters with higher densities did not mix with warmer sea- waters.

Oceanographers divide the oceans into horizontal and vertical zones. The photic zone extends from the surface to about 200 m deep, where there is enough light for photosynthesis to occur. Some of the organic matter created by photosynthesis is consumed by ocean creatures. The remainder, as well as other ocean organisms, sink into deep ocean waters out of contact with the atmosphere. The sinking then removes them from the carbon cycle, which eventually transfers into sedimentary rocks.

The sediment in the first few centimeters of the ocean floor is loaded with dead and live organisms and plants, as well as aerobic (oxygen-breathing) microorganisms. The aerobic microorganisms use all the available oxygen in the seafloor plus the oxygen in the subseafloor. Anaerobic methanogens (nonoxygen-breathing microorganisms that produce methane) occur in the oxygen-depleted, organic-bearing subseafloor and produce methane. The methane is either used as energy by other anaerobic organisms (methane-eating methanotrophs) or becomes trapped as gas hydrates (clathrates).

Methane clathrates are cages of water molecules that trap single molecules of methane. Significant reservoirs of methane clathrates have been found in arctic and Antarctic permafrost and along continental margins beneath the ocean floor. The deposits of methane clathrates are a potential source of methane, as well as a potential contributor to global warming. Some climate models suggest that today's methane occurrence and emission from the ocean floor is similar to the type of occurrence and emission that may have happened to produce the significant carbon dioxide increase during the Paleocene-Eocene Thermal Maximum around 56 million years ago. As mentioned on page 11, *A friend, Gerry MacMillan, described a PBS - TV program that showed small, isolated craters which were produced by natural explosions of local hydrate methane deposits in permafrost in northern Russia and Alaska.*

Tidal currents, wind and ocean currents continuously circulate the water in the oceans and redistribute the temperatures, pollutants, salinity, carbon dioxide, etc., and have a significant impact on global climate.

Water evaporates from the oceans, and at any given time, about 20×10^{12} tonnes of water vapor is in the atmosphere. When clouds of warm air laden with moisture meet cooler air, the moisture condenses into droplets and falls as precipitation. Normally, about 78 % of global precipitation occurs over the oceans.

Floods and global warming

As the air gets warmer, it holds more moisture and produces overloaded clouds. Downpours occur when the overloaded clouds meet cold air. These actions produce flooding with a quick runoff of water that does not wet to soil deeply. This causes rivers to rise quickly and land depressions to become lakes. Most of the flooding occurs within 100 km of shore, although some major storms occur far inland.

On November 14 and 15, 2021, violent floods occurred over a large area about 50 to 150 km inland from the ocean in southwestern British Columbia, Canada. They caused landslides that killed 5 persons and cut off roads and railroads from Metro Vancouver and the rest of Canada for several weeks. Part of the city of Abbotsford, which had been built in a low-lying area, became a temporary lake. It is noteworthy that a major forest fire occurred in the area earlier that summer, in July 2021, and burned the underbrush and rubble, which left relatively bare soil. The bare soil was amenable to wetting which made it susceptible to landslides in the mountainous region (see the section on forest fires).

Hurricanes *(transcribed from NASA Science report, "How do Hurricanes form")* Hurricanes are like giant engines that use warm, moist air as fuel. That is why they form only over warm ocean waters near the equator. The warm, moist air over the ocean rises upward from near the ocean surface. This air moves up and away and leaves an ocean surface with lower air pressure. Air from the surrounding areas with higher pressure pushes into a low-pressure area. Then the "new" air becomes warm and moist, and it rises. As the warm air continues to rise, the surrounding air swirls in to take its place. As the warm moist air rises and cools off, the water in the air forms clouds. The whole system of winds and clouds spins and grows. Fed by the ocean's heat and water evaporating from the surface.

An eye develops in the center of the storm as it rotates ever faster. It is very calm and clear in the eye, with very low pressure. Higher pressure from above flows down into the eye.

Hurricanes usually weaken when they reach land because they are no longer being fed by the energy from the warm ocean waters. However, they often move far inland, dumping many inches of rain and producing strong winds and water damage before they die out completely. Recently, hurricanes seem to have become stronger, more severe and produce more damage on land than previous years.

Tornados, Thunderstorms, and lightning

A *tornado* is a violently rotating column of air that is in contact with both the earth's surface and cumulonimbus clouds. Tornadoes are often visible in the form of a funnel originating from the base of a cloud. The winds blow clockwise in the southern hemisphere when viewed from the surface of the planet and counterclockwise in the northern hemisphere. Most tornadoes are about 80m across, and the wind speeds in them are generally less than 180 km/h. However, extreme tornadoes were more than 3 km in diameter, attained speeds of 480 km/h, and stayed on the ground for more than 100km. The USA and Canada have more tornadoes than any other country. Most occur in the central and southeastern USA, colloquially known as Tornado valley. Tornadoes in Canada tend to occur in the central and southern parts of the country. (Wikipedia, September 13, 2022).

Thunderstorms are characterized by the presence of lightning and the acoustic effect in the earth's atmosphere. They occur in a type of cloud known as Cumulonimbus, are usually accompanied by strong winds, and often produce heavy rain. Severe thunderstorms are a dangerous weather phenomenon as they are often associated with strong winds, tornadoes, and lightning. Thunderstorms develop through a rapid upward movement of warm, moist air. As the warm, moist air moves upward, it cools, condenses, and forms Cumulonimbus clouds. When the clouds reach a dew point temperature, the water vapor condenses into droplets or ice and falls to the ground pulling the cool air with it. Occasionally it causes strong winds. (Wikipedia, September 13, 2022)

Lightning commonly occurs during thunderstorms or other types of energetic weather systems. It is a naturally occurring electrostatic discharge during which two electrically charged regions temporarily neutralize themselves and cause an instantaneous release of a gigajoule of energy. (Wikipedia, September 13, 2022).

In July 2022, part of a herd of cattle in Mankola, Saskatchewan, was startled by a major thunderstorm and rushed to get away. They were stopped by a wire fence.

Lightning struck the wire fence and killed the entire runaway herd of 28 cattle, including 14 cows, the herd bull, and calves. (Bonnie Allen, C.B.C. News, Jul. 13, 2022, 12:43 p.m. C.T.)

Blizzards

Blizzards are heavy precipitation events that occur in winter.

FRESHWATER

The remaining 2.5 % of the water on the planet is fresh water and is distributed as follows:

- about 1.7225 % is in ice and permanent snow cover in the Antarctic, arctic, Greenland and mountain glaciers,
- about 0.77 % is groundwater,
- about 0.0075 % is in lakes, reservoirs, and river systems.

ATMOSPHERE (AIR.)

The earth's atmosphere, commonly known as air, contains approximately 900 gigatonnes of carbon as carbon dioxide and methane. It consists of layers of gases that are retained by earth's gravity and surround the planet. The atmosphere protects life on earth by:

- creating pressure for liquid water to exist on the earth's surface,
- absorbing ultraviolet solar radiation,
- warming the surface through heat retention (greenhouse gases),
- reducing temperature extremes between day and night.

The atmosphere becomes thinner with increasing altitude, and the air pressure and density decrease with increasing altitude. The temperature in the atmosphere has a detailed profile and provides a means for distinguishing atmospheric layers. The earth's atmosphere can be divided into five layers: troposphere, stratosphere, mesosphere, thermosphere and exosphere. There is no definite boundary between the atmosphere and outer space. The Kármán line, at 100 km (62 miles), is often used as the border, but the outermost edge of earth's atmosphere is the outer edge of the exosphere at about 10,000 km (6,200 miles).

Troposphere

The troposphere is the lowest layer and extends from the earth's surface to an average height of 12 km (7.5 miles). It contains roughly 80 % of the mass of the earth's atmosphere and is the layer where most of the earth's weather takes place. It has basically all the weather-associated cloud types. The temperature in the troposphere declines with increasing altitude, as the troposphere is mostly heated through energy transfer at the earth's surface. Furthermore, at higher altitudes, the molecules are further apart, and adiabatic cooling occurs. Most conventional aviation takes place in the troposphere. The top of the troposphere is bounded by a tropopause which is a boundary where the cold air of the troposphere meets the warm atmosphere of the overlying stratosphere.

Table 1
Composition of earth's atmosphere

Nitrogen (N)	78.08 %	
Oxygen (O)	20.95 %	
Argon (Ar)	0.93 %	
Carbon dioxide (CO_2)	0.0416 %	Greenhouse gas

Neon (Ne)	0.00182 %	
Methane (CH4)	0.000187 %	Greenhouse gas
Helium (He)	0.00052 %	
Krypton (Kr)	0.00011 %	
Hydrogen (H)	0.00005 %	
Xenon (Xe)	0.0000087 %	
Ozone (O_3)	0.000007 %	Greenhouse gas
Nitrous oxide (NO_2)	0.000002 %	Greenhouse gas
Water vapor	usually 1 to 3% (up to 5%)	Greenhouse gas

Stratosphere

The stratosphere is the second layer of the earth's atmosphere and extends from the top of the tropopause at about 12 km (7.5 miles) to about 50 to 55 km (31 to 34 miles) above the earth. It contains the ozone layer, which absorbs ultraviolet radiation from the sun and warms the stratosphere. Turbulence and mixing are restricted in the stratosphere, so the top of the stratosphere is much warmer than the bottom. The pressure at the top is only 1/1000 the pressure at sea level as the molecules are much further apart than at sea level. The stratosphere is the highest layer that can be accessed by jet-powered aircraft.

Mesosphere

The mesosphere is the third highest layer of the earth's atmosphere. It extends from about 51 km (31 miles) to the mesopause at 80 to 85 km (50 to 53 miles) above the earth's surface. The temperature in the mesosphere drops with increasing altitude, and the mesopause is the coldest place on earth with an average temperature of -85°C. The air is so cold that scarce water sublimates into polar-mesospheric noctilucent (phosphorescent) clouds. Most meteors burn up in the mesosphere upon entrance into the earth's atmosphere. The mesosphere is accessed by rocket-powered aircraft.

Thermosphere

The thermosphere extends from mesopause at about 80 km (50 miles) above the earth to about 500 to 1000 km (310 to 620 miles). The temperature of the thermosphere gradually increases with height and can rise to as high as 1500°C. The temperature, in the usual sense, is not meaningful because the air is so rarified that an individual molecule travels about 1 kilometer between collisions with other molecules. This layer is cloudless and free of water vapor, and contains the ionosphere. Aurora borealis are occasionally seen in this layer. The International Space Station and many satellites orbit in this layer.

Exosphere

The exosphere is the outermost layer of the earth's atmosphere and extends to about 10,000 km (6,200 miles) above the earth's surface, where it merges into the solar wind. The layer is mainly composed of low-density elements, hydrogen, and helium, but contains several heavy molecules, including nitrogen, oxygen and carbon dioxide. The atoms and molecules are so far apart that they can travel hundreds of kilometers without colliding with one another. Aurora borealis sometimes occur in the lower part of the exosphere, and many satellites orbit in this layer.

Ionosphere

The ionosphere is a region of the atmosphere that is ionized by solar radiation and is responsible for auroras. It stretches from 50 to 1,000 km (31 to 621 miles) and includes the mesosphere, thermosphere and parts of the exosphere. Ionization in the mesosphere essentially ceases during the night, so auroras are typically seen only in the thermosphere and lower exosphere.

Nitrogen

Nitrogen is the most abundant element in the earth's atmosphere and the 30th most abundant in the earth's crust at 19 parts per million (0.0019 %). It is element 7 of the periodic table of elements with symbol N and atomic weight 14.0067. Nitrogen is a constituent of all living matter on earth and forms about 3 % of the human body. It is a critical element for plant production and is a major component of chlorophyll as the most crucial pigment for photosynthesis. It is largely an inert, colorless, odorless and tasteless gas and has many uses, such as ammonia (NH_3), fertilizer, liquid nitrogen refrigerant, nitric acid, etc.

Oxygen

Oxygen is:

- The second most abundant element in the earth's atmosphere,
- the third most abundant element in the universe and the sun (about 0.9 % of the sun) after hydrogen and helium,
- the most abundant element in the earth's crust at 46.1 % by volume (49.2 % by mass).
- A principal constituent of most rock-forming minerals in the earth's crust,
- part of all living organisms and life forms on earth.
- A constituent of every organ, muscle, and bone in the human body.
- About 65 % of the human body.

Oxygen is element 8 of the periodic table of elements with the symbol O and atomic weight 16. It is a highly reactive element and is an oxidizing agent that readily forms oxides with most elements and compounds. The reactions produced by oxygen combining with other elements and compounds provide energy and respiration to the molecules in living organisms and uses-up the oxygen in the atmosphere. In particular, a human adult at rest inhales about 1.8 to 2.4 grams of oxygen per minute. More than 6 billion tons of oxygen are inhaled by humanity per year. Oxygen is too chemically reactive to remain a free element in the air without being continuously replenished. According to some estimates, the photosynthesis of green algae and cyanobacteria in oceans provides about 70 % of the free oxygen on earth, and photosynthesis on terrestrial plants provides about 30 %. A simplified formula for photosynthesis (reproduced from page 5) is:

$$6\ CO_2 + 6\ H_2O + photons = C_6H_{12}O_6 + 6O_2$$

or simply

carbon dioxide + water + sunlight = glucose + oxygen (free element)

Earth is unusual in the solar system by having such a high concentration of oxygen (20.95 % O_2) in its atmosphere. Mars has 0.1 % oxygen, and Venus has less.

Free oxygen was almost nonexistent in the earth's atmosphere during the first billion years of the earth's existence (4.6 to 3.5 billion years ago (bya)). Photosynthetic bacteria evolved about 3.5 bya, and their presence is embedded in seabed rock. It appears as significant quantities of red iron oxides, which were likely created by iron-oxidizing anaerobic (non-oxygen breathing) bacteria.

By about 2.4 billion years ago, large amounts of free oxygen had developed by photosynthesis in the oceans and atmosphere and created The Great Oxygenation Event, which caused the near extinction of anaerobic bacteria and enabled aerobic (oxygen-breathing) bacteria to produce cellular respiration by using free oxygen in living cells, including complex multicellular organisms such as plants and animals.

Free oxygen reached 10 % of the present level around 1.7 billion years ago.

Since the beginning of the Cambrian period (541 million years ago), the oxygen levels in the atmosphere have fluctuated between 15 % and 30 % (figure 9). Toward the end of the Carboniferous period (about 300 million years ago), oxygen levels in the atmosphere reached a maximum of 35 %, which probably contributed to the growth of giant insects, animals, and plants.

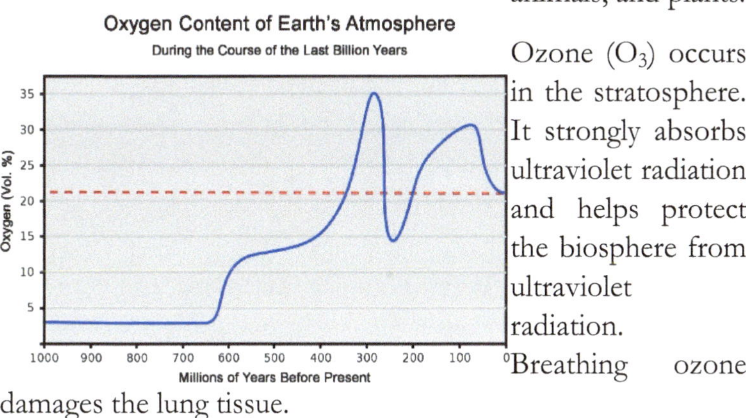

Ozone (O_3) occurs in the stratosphere. It strongly absorbs ultraviolet radiation and helps protect the biosphere from ultraviolet radiation. Breathing ozone damages the lung tissue.

Carbon Dioxide (CO_2)

Carbon dioxide is the primary source of life on earth and the primary cause of global warming. It is a colorless gas that sublimates to dry ice at -78.5 °C and is non-toxic at low concentrations. It is present in the atmosphere, oceans, rivers, lakes, glaciers, wetlands, and groundwater. The following characteristics of carbon dioxide are described elsewhere in this paper:

(1) *Photosynthesis*: Plants, algae and cyanobacteria use the carbon dioxide from the atmosphere and oceans for photosynthesis to produce carbohydrates in plants + free oxygen in the atmosphere. In turn, all aerobic organisms (bacteria, plants, animals, etc.) consume carbohydrates and oxygen for growth, energy and respiration and exhale some carbon dioxide.

(2) *Greenhouse gas:* Carbon dioxide is a major greenhouse gas, and it produces global warming. It does this by trapping specific photons of energy from the atmosphere before they pass into space. Then the carbon dioxide emits the energy of each photon into the atmosphere by radiation for years before it releases the photon into space or back into the atmosphere.

Carbon dioxide is continuously added to and removed from the atmosphere and oceans by natural processes (see part 1). Recently, humans began adding carbon dioxide to the atmosphere by using the carbon that was stored as hydrocarbons in the rocks for millions of years. Hence, the atmospheric carbon dioxide content increased from about 280 ppm in pre-industrial levels to about 417 ppm at present.

Carbon cycle experts estimated that the natural sinks (photosynthesis on land and in oceans plus limestone deposited from oceans) absorbed all the carbon dioxide that was produced by natural processes plus about half of the carbon dioxide that was emitted by humans each year during the 2010-2020 decade (Global Carbon Update, 2021). Hence, about half of the carbon dioxide produced by humans causes global warming.

A modern record of atmospheric carbon dioxide began at the Mauna Loa Observatory in Hawaii in 1958. The atmospheric carbon dioxide in1960 was about 320 ppm, and the annual input was about 0.8 ppm. By 2021 the atmospheric carbon dioxide had increased to 414.72 ppm, and the annual input reached 2.4 ppm some years. By June 2022, the carbon dioxide input jumped 2.58 ppm over the 2021 amount. Hence, the atmospheric carbon dioxide concentrations are increasing, mostly because humans are burning fossil fuels for energy by processes that combine carbon with free oxygen and produce carbon dioxide (CO_2).

The more we overshoot what natural processes can remove each year, the faster the atmospheric concentration of carbon dioxide rises. The rise that occurred during the 2010-2020 decade is greater than the rise that occurred at the end of the last ice age when the glaciers began melting (11,000 - 17,000 years ago) (Lindsey, 2022).

It is noteworthy that during the glaciation period of 800,000 years (see Figure 2b, The EPICA ice core project), the atmospheric carbon dioxide content did not exceed 300 ppm, but now it is 417 ppm.

The last time that the atmospheric carbon dioxide was higher than 400 was during the "Mid-Pliocene Warm Period" 3.3 million years ago. At that time, the average global temperatures were 2.5- 4 °C warmer than during the pre-industrial era (Lindsey, 2022) and 10 to 20 °C warmer in the high latitudes (Wikipedia). The sea levels were at least 16 feet higher (Lindsey, 2022) than in 1990.

Toxicity of Carbon gases
- Carbon monoxide is poisonous.
- Carbon dioxide is non-toxic at low concentrations. Currently, the carbon dioxide content in the atmosphere is about 0.0417 %
- At 1 to 2 %, it may make some people feel drowsy and their lungs feel stuffy.
- At 7 to 10 %, it may cause dizziness, headache, visual and hearing dysfunction, suffocation and unconsciousness within a few minutes to an hour.

Carbon dioxide gas is heavier than air, and high concentrations can develop in pockets.

Methane

Methane (CH_4) is a chemical compound and is the main constituent of natural gas, which is used as a fuel for homes, automobiles, and industry. As a fuel, it produces more energy per mass than any other hydrocarbon due to its relatively large hydrogen content. This happens because hydrogen accounts for only 25 % of the molecular mass of methane but produces 55 % of the heat of the combustion of methane.

Methane was formed by geological and biological processes and occurs in (1) the earth's crust, (2) under the sea floor, (3) in wetlands and (4) in ruminants. Some methane escapes into the atmosphere from decaying organic material in wetlands, from ruminants, and from pipelines and preparations for distribution. The concentration of atmospheric methane has increased by about 156% Since 1750 AD.

The methane in the earth's crust is referred to as organic thermogenic methane, inorganic methane, and biogenic methane. The organic thermogenic methane occurs in sedimentary strata as it is produced by metamorphism at elevated temperatures and pressures from organic material in sedimentary rocks. The inorganic methane was produced from inorganic compounds without biological activity and occurred in crystalline rocks that were deposited from magma at depth. Biogenic methane occurs in soils, ruminants (cattle, chickens, pigs), guts of termites, and oxygen-depleted sediments below seafloors, lake bottoms, and rice fields.

Organic thermogenic methane is the main source of natural gas. It occurs in oil wells, coal deposits, natural gas deposits and shale gas (Figure 10).

Organic Thermogenic methane

The methane associated with producing oil wells occurs at the top of oil as natural gas. It was initially viewed as a by-product, as a hazard, and as a disposal problem until pipelines and storage facilities were constructed to deliver it to consumer markets. Consequently, most of the natural gas was initially released into the atmosphere or burned off at the oil fields. Now, unwanted natural gas is often returned to reservoirs while waiting for future markets. Natural gas consists of methane and contains small percentages of carbon dioxide, nitrogen, hydrogen, sulfide, and helium. These elements and compounds must be removed before transportation to prevent the corrosion of pipelines. Natural gas is colorless and odorless, so a sulfur smell is usually added for detection.

Natural gas also occurs in coal beds as coal bed methane. It escapes readily from the coal horizons and is a cause of explosions in coal mines. For example, CBC recently (late 2021) reported that an explosion in a coal mine killed 52 miners and rescuers underground (name withheld for privacy). The explosion was caused by methane which filled the mine with toxic fumes and prevented rescue efforts for some time. Eventually, 239 miners were rescued from the underground.

The world's largest natural gas field is the offshore South Pars/ North Dome Gas Condensate field that is shared between Iran and Qatar. Other large proven natural

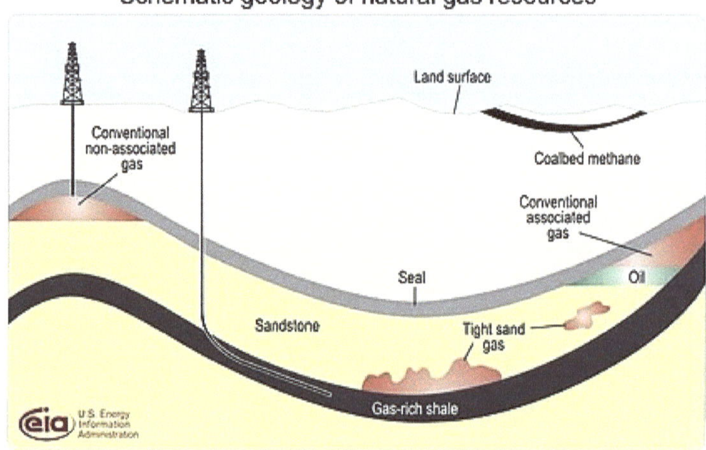

gas deposits are in Russia, Iran, Qatar, Turkmenistan, and the USA. One of the world's largest and least known natural gas deposit is near the village of Darvaza in Turkmenistan. Reportedly, the ground above it collapsed, swallowed a drill rig, and created a crater about 70 meters (230 feet) in diameter and 20 meters (66 feet) deep. The escaping natural gas was purposefully set on fire in 1971 and is still burning. It has become a tourist attraction as the **"Door to Hell"** or **"Gates of Hell"** (See Figure 7). Obviously, the continuous burning of the natural gas in the Darvaza crater since 1971 has deposited enormous amounts of carbon dioxide into the atmosphere.

Figure 10: (reproduced from Wikipedia report on "Natural gas").

Considerable resources of methane occur as shale gas

in sedimentary rocks, especially in USA and Canada. Shale gas requires artificially created fractures by hydraulic fracturing (fracking) to allow the gas to flow. The procedure involves drilling vertically to the natural gas bearing horizon, then pointing the drill to follow the horizon horizontally for hundreds or thousands of feet. Water mixed with a variety of chemicals is forced through the wellbore casing. The high-pressure water breaks up the rock and releases natural gas.

Biogenic methane

Some of the earth's methane is biogenic and is produced by methanogenesis, which is a form of anaerobic respiration by non-oxygen breathing methanogens (microorganisms that produce methane). The methanogens occupy landfills, soils, ruminants (cattle, chickens, pigs), guts of termites, and oxygen-depleted sediments below seafloors, lake bottoms, and rice fields. Ruminants belch methane, accounting for about 22 % of US annual methane emissions to the atmosphere.

Seafloor methane

The sediments in the first few centimeters of the seafloor are enriched in the oxygen that aerobic microorganisms (oxygen breathing) remove from the subseafloor. Anaerobic methanogens in the oxygen-depleted, carbon-bearing subseafloor produce methane that is either used as energy by other anaerobic organisms, especially methane-eating methanotrophs or becomes trapped as gas hydrates (clathrates). The methane-eating methanotrophs are the reason why little of the methane generated at depth reaches the ocean surface.

Methane clathrates are cages of water molecules that trap single molecules of methane. Significant reservoirs of methane clathrates have been found in the Arctic and Antarctic permafrost and along continental margins beneath the ocean floor in the polar regions. Methane clathrates can form from biogenic and thermogenic methane. The deposits of methane clathrates are a potential source of methane, as well as a potential contributor to global warming.

Greenhouse gas

The earth's atmospheric methane accounts for about 20 % of the global warming due to long-lived greenhouse gases (i.e., carbon dioxide (CO_2), methane (CH_4), nitrous oxide (N_2O), ozone (O_3) and chlorofluorocarbons (CFCs)). The atmospheric methane concentration has increased 156 % since around 1750 AD and is currently 1866 ppb. For comparison, the percentage increase of other greenhouse gases is about 47 % for carbon dioxide and 23 % for nitrous oxide. Historic atmospheric methane concentrations ranged between 300 and 400 ppb during glacial periods and between 600 and 700 ppb during the warm interglacial periods.

FOREST FIRES

Forest fires create large amounts of greenhouse gases, and their effects extend beyond killing trees and burning the underbrush. According to a CBC television program, "The Nature of Things," on May 28, 2022, the heat of Global warming dries forests and makes them susceptible to becoming forest fires. The chance of a lightning strike that starts forest fires increases with every degree of global warming. The best prevention of forest fires is early detection and immediate firefighting to prevent the fire from spreading beyond the size of a football field. When a fire spreads beyond this size, it becomes a problematic forest fire.

Recently, the frequency and severity of forest fires have increased, and sometimes, firefighters have been unable to divert them from towns. In particular:

- In 2016, the city of Fort McMurray, Alberta, was largely destroyed by a forest fire, and the residents were evacuated.
- In 2017, British Columbia experienced one of the worst forest fire seasons, and many rural homes and first nation homes were destroyed in the town of

Boston Flats, BC.

- In 2018, the town of Paradise and the surrounding villages in California were destroyed by the worst raging forest fire ever experienced in northern California.
- In 2021, the town of Lytton, B.C. and residential areas throughout south-central and southeastern British Columbia was destroyed by forest fires that were more brutal and severe than those of 2017 BC. Forest fires. The fires burned the underbrush leaving relatively bare soil on the mountain slopes. Four months later, heavy rains washed the bare soil and produced landslides that covered several highways and killed five people (see Chapter 3, floods and global warming, page 19).

The above-mentioned forest fires burned large tracts of forest and created immense amounts of greenhouse gases. Dr. Krutz, a Senior Research Scientist with Natural Resources Canada, reported that about 1.2 million hectares of forest were burned in British Columbia in 2017, and about 1.3 million hectares and counting were burned in 2021. The unofficial estimate by the Pacific Institute for Climate Solutions (PICS) is that the area burned by the forest fires in 2017 is more than 15 times the average yearly area burned in the province between 1990 to 2015 and that the direct emissions of greenhouse gases from the 2017 fires are about two to three times the emissions from fossil fuel burning from all sectors in BC.

A Consortium of the University of Victoria's Pacific Climate Impacts (PCIC) and Environment and Climate Change Canada (ECCC) suggested that the November 2021 British Columbia flood described in the section "flood and global warming" was due to human-induced climate change. Another impact of forest fires on the atmosphere is that the trees killed by the fires will decompose over the next decades and release more carbon dioxide into the atmosphere. In addition, the trees killed by the forest fires will not be removing carbon dioxide from the atmosphere by photosynthesis as they would if they were still living trees.

Researchers have also found that severe forest fires propel smoke, soot, and fine particulate matter into the top of the troposphere and lower parts of the stratosphere, where it resides temporarily. Atmospheric models suggest that these concentrations of sooty particles could increase the absorption of incoming solar radiation during winter months by as much as 15 %.

Causes of Forest Fires
- Natural causes, lightning.
- Man-made causes, carelessness, and ignorance about forest fires.
- Fires due to the collection of dry forest products and litter.
- Fires due to logging operations.
- Fires due to industrial operations in forests.

Additional damage from Forest fires
- Destruction of seeds.
- Destruction of young seedlings.
- Damage to young plants and trees.
- Injury to wildlife.
- Deterioration of site.
- Others

Control of Forest Fires
- Early detection and firefighting of fires.
- Removal of forest litter along the forest boundary.
- Create fire breaks where possible.
- Close surveillance and control of fires during forest fire seasons.

Drought

A drought is an event of prolonged shortages in the water supply (such as below-average precipitation, excessive evaporation, or lack of groundwater. Humans have often tried to explain droughts as either a natural disaster, a disaster caused by humans, or the result of supernatural forces. Dry periods can occur randomly or periodically and last for weeks, months or years without apparent causes. Periods of heat can significantly worsen drought conditions by hastening the evaporation of water vapor. Dry seasons increase the chances of developing drought and increase the probability of forest fires.

During El Nino, some parts of the world are drier and hotter than average, and the winters are warmer.
Human activities such as irrigation, deforestation and erosion adversely impact the ability of the land to capture and hold water. Combined with global warming, they may produce drought.

The Atacama Desert in Chile, which lasted 400 years, is an example of the most prolonged drought ever recorded in history.
An example of cyclic droughts is provided by Palliser's triangle, which covers southwestern Saskatchewan and southeastern Alberta. The region was arid when Palliser explored it in 1857, but it soon became a grassland for buffalo and, by 1910, was settled by farmers opening the west. From about 1932 to 1935, it was a dust bowl due to lack of rain and, probably to a small extent, poor farming practices, which were quickly modified and adapted to the land and seasons. Nevertheless, since 1940, every decade has had at least one dry year, presumably due to the physiography of the mountains to the west. In 2021, an -80-year cycle (1857 to 1934, 1935 to 2021) was fulfilled by an exceedingly dry year.

ICE AGES: GLACIAL AND INTERGLACIAL PERIODS

There have been five or six ice ages on earth in the past 3 billion years, six if the first ice age that is poorly documented is included. Most of the ice ages had a few glacial and interglacial periods. We are presently in an interglacial period of the Quaternary sub-ice age that began 2.58 million years ago (mya) and had many glaciations that consisted of glacial and interglacial periods (see part 1 of this paper). During the last 800,000 years, there were eight glaciations that lasted an average of 100,000 years per glaciation. The interglacial periods within the glaciations lasted between 10,000 and 15,000 years; the longest one lasted 28,000 years. According to research published in Nature Science, the current interglacial period is expected to end and the next glacial period to begin within 1,500 years. However, due to the current emissions of greenhouse gases, the current warm climate may last another 23,000 to 50,000 years or even 100,000 years. The table below shows the known ice ages on earth.

ICE AGE

Age (million years ago)	Ice Age (name)	Geologic Age	Glaciation (name, age)	Comments
2,900 - 2,780	Pongola	Archean		associated with outgassing
2,400 - 2,100	Huron	Paleoproterozoic		
770 - 547	Snowball Earth	Neoproterozoic	Sturt, (715-680) Marino, (650-635) Gaskiers, (580- ?) Baykour, (?-547)	the warmest temperature on earth occurred in the inter-glacial period 550 to 750 mya.
450 - 420	Late Ordovician glaciation	Ordovician, Silurian		
360 - 260	Karoo			

34 - present	Late Cenozoic ice age	Late Paleogene, Neogene, Holocene	Quaternary (2.58 - present)	

Huron Ice Age

The Huron ice age (2,400 - 2,100 million years ago (mya)) was probably caused by the elimination of atmospheric methane, a greenhouse gas, and coincided with the Great Oxygenation Event that occurred about 2,400 mya. The Oxygenation Event happened when there was too much oxygen in deep photic zones of oceans for the survival of anaerobic bacteria that were part an early photosynthesis, which evolved about 3.5 mya. However, the oxygen content was suitable for the aerobic cyanobacteria (living organisms) that were in shallower parts of photic zones and were the beginning of current photosynthesis on earth's atmosphere.

Snowball Ice Age

The Snowball ice age appears to have been the most severe ice age on earth and may have been initiated by a reduction in atmospheric CO_2. The first two glaciation periods of the Snowball ice age (Sturt, 715-680 mya and Marino, 650-635 mya) reportedly covered the entire planet, including the equator, with ice and snow. The interglacial period between them was probably the warmest period ever on earth. The Snowball ice age ended about 550 mya with the Cambrian Explosion, which was a major volcanic outgassing of carbon dioxide and produced an extremely high carbon dioxide atmosphere. It has been suggested that the explosion was a reaction to the extremely cold ice age.

Late Ordovician Glaciation

A minor series of glaciations occurred from 460 to 420 mya.

Karoo Ice Age

The evolution of land plants in the Devonian period (419 mya to 359 mya) caused an increase in planetary oxygen levels and a reduction of CO_2, which resulted in a late Paleozoic ice age. It was named Karoo glaciation as it was found in the Karoo region in South Africa. The Smithsonian data (figure 5) indicates that there were at least 5 interglacial periods during Karoo ice age. Other data in this report show that the oxygen levels fluctuated between 15 % and 30 % and reached 35 % at one point. The ice age ended shortly before earth's most severe known extinction event, "The Permian- Triassic Extinction Event." The event killed most marine and some terrestrial life due to complex volcanic, anaerobic, and other activities that produced high carbon dioxide, methanogenic methane, very high temperatures, fungal spikes and other conditions for a few million years (see Figure 5). The dinosaurs evolved during this time.

Late Cenozoic Ice Age

The Late Cenozoic ice age began in the Antarctic 34 mya and continued to present. The first 30 million years mostly involved the Antarctic. The Quaternary Sub-Ice Age, is part of the Late Cenozoic ice age. It started 2.58 mya in North America. Numerous ice sheets extended over parts of Europe, China, North America and Antarctic. During the last 800,000 years of the Quaternary Sub-Ice-Age, cycles of glacial-interglacial glaciations occurred at about 100,000-year intervals. The last interval began about 110,000 years ago and ended about 12,000 years ago. The glacial period within this last interval began 26,000 years ago and ended about 12,000 years ago. It is noteworthy that during the preceding seven interglacial periods, the atmospheric carbon dioxide content did not exceed 300 ppm (See figure 2). Whereas during the current interglacial period it is already 418 ppm. As indicated in the section on Carbon dioxide the current interglacial period could continue up to 50,000 more years, due to current global warming. Research evidence in 2009 has indicated that electromagnetic radiation from the sun may have been an initial cause for earth to warm after an ice age.

SUN

The characteristics of the sun, described by Wikipedia, are summarized here to determine if there is a relationship between solar activities and global warming. The sun and its solar system, including earth, formed about 4.6 billion years ago from a gravitational collapse of matter in a giant molecular cloud. The central mass became so hot that it initiated nuclear fusion in its core. It fuses about 600 million tons of hydrogen into helium every second, converting 4 million tons into energy, and is the source of the sun's light and heat. The energy of the sunlight supports almost all life on earth through photosynthesis and drives the earth's climate and weather.

Over the past 4.6 billion years, the proportion of helium at the core has increased from 24% to 60 % due to the fusion of hydrogen into helium. An inner core of helium has begun to form. Helium will continue to accumulate at the core, and in about 5 billion years, the build-up will cause the sun to exit the main sequence and become a red giant that will engulf the current orbits of Mercury and Venus and will be too hot for life on earth.

Characteristics of the Sun
- Diameter = 1.39 million Kilometers (109 times earth)
- Mass = 330,000 times earth, 99.86 % of the mass of the entire solar system,
- Distance (sun's center to earth's center) =150,000,000 km; 93,000,000 miles (one astronomical unit).
- No definite boundary since the sun is a gas. However, the sun's radius is from its center to the edge of the photosphere (the sun's outer layer).
- Heat transfer: by radiation from the sun's core to 0.7 radii, then by convection to the photosphere.

Current composition of photosphere:

Hydrogen = 73.46 %

Helium = 24.85 %

Oxygen = 0.77 %

Carbon = 0.29 %

Iron = 0.16 %

Neon = 0.12 %

Nitrogen = 0.09 %

Silicon = 0. 07 %

Magnesium =0.05 %

Sulfer =0.04 %

The sunlight at the top of the earth's atmosphere is composed of about 50 % infrared light, 40 % visible light and 10 % ultraviolet light. The solar constant is the amount of power that the sun deposits per unit area that is directly exposed to sunlight. The solar constant in the earth's outer atmosphere is about 1,368 W/m2 and about 1,000 W/m2 at the earth's surface. Over 70 % of the solar ultraviolet radiation is filtered out by the earth's atmosphere. The solar ultraviolet radiation ionizes earth's upper atmosphere creating an electrically conductive ionosphere.

Structure of the sun

The sun is a gaseous object that consists of a Core, Radiative zone, Tachocline, Convective zone, and photosphere, and is surrounded by an atmosphere that consists of the Chromosphere, Solar Transition region, Corona and Heliosphere. The visible parts are the "photosphere" and "atmosphere." The photosphere is seen as the sun. The sun's atmosphere can be seen only when the sun is hidden, as during a solar eclipse. To prevent blindness, special precautions are required for watching a solar eclipse.

Core

The core is the innermost 20-25% of the sun's radius. It has a density of up to 150 g/cm3 (about 150 times the density of water) and sufficient pressure and temperature (about 15.7 million K) to produce 99 % of the sun's thermal energy by nuclear fusion. The thermal energy is transferred outwards from the core through many successive layers of the sun and escapes into space through radiation of photons, which are quantum of light that carry energy but zero rest mass. The sun releases energy at the mass-energy conversion rate of 4.26 million metric tons per second (which requires 600 metric megatons of hydrogen). The enormous power output of the sun is due to the huge size and density of the core. Recent data indicates that the core and reactive zone rotate faster than the zone above.

Radiative zone

The energy is transferred from the core by thermal radiation through a radiative zone that extends from the core to about 0.7 of the solar radii.

Tachocline

The radiative zone is separated from a convective zone by a transition layer, the Tacholine, which is a region of a sharp regime change between the uniform rotation of the radiative zone and a differential rotation of a convection zone, resulting in a significant shear as the successive layers slide past one another. It is hypothesized that a magnetic dynamo within this layer generates the sun's magnetic field.

Convective zone

The sun's convection zone extends from 0.7 radii to near the surface. The solar plasma in this layer is not dense enough or hot enough to transfer the heat energy via radiation, but its density is low enough to allow convective currents to develop and move the sun's energy outward toward its surface.

Photosphere

The photosphere is the layer of the sun that we see. It is tens to hundreds of kilometers thick and radiates solar energy at 5,777 ° K. The photons produced in this layer escape the sun through a transparent atmosphere, and it becomes solar radiation sunlight.

Atmosphere

During a total solar eclipse, when the disk of the sun is covered by the moon, parts of the sun's atmosphere can be seen.

The coolest layer is a minimum temperature region extending about 500 km above the photosphere. Its temperature is about 4,100 °K.

Chromosphere

The chromosphere is about 2,000 km thick. Its temperature increases gradually to about 20,000 °K at the top, where helium becomes partly ionized.

Solar Transition region

A 200 km thick transition region occurs above the chromosphere where the temperature rises to 1,000 000 °K. The temperature increase causes full ionization of the helium in the region and reduces the radiative cooling of the plasma.

Corona

The next layer is the corona which has a large volume. The average temperature of the corona and the solar wind is 1,000 000 - 2,000 000 °K; however, in the hottest region, it is 8,000 000 - 20,000 000 °K. Some of its heat is known to be from magnetic reconnection.

Heliosphere

The heliosphere is the outermost atmosphere of the sun and is filled with solar wind plasma.

It is about 20 times the thickness of the solar radii.

Photons and Neutrinos

The photons released in the core are almost immediately absorbed by the solar plasma in the radiative zone. Re-emission happens in a random direction at slightly lower energy. This sequence of emissions and absorptions takes a long time for radiation to reach the sun's surface. Some estimates range from 10,000 to 170,000 years.

It takes neutrinos, which account for 2 % of the total energy production, 2.3 seconds to reach the surface of the sun. Neutrinos are also released by fusion actions in the core, but unlike photons, they rarely interact with matter, so they can escape the sun immediately.

Magnetic field

The sun has a magnetic field that varies across its surface. Concentrations of the magnetic field appear as dark patches on the sun's photosphere, which indicates that they are cool areas. At a solar minimum, few solar spots are visible, whereas at maximum solar sunspots occur close to the solar equator. The largest sunspots can be tens of thousands of kilometers across.

The sunspots are part of an 11- year sunset cycle that is half of a 22 - year dynamo cycle that corresponds to an oscillatory exchange of energy between the internal and external solar magnetic fields. At a solar maximum, the external field is at minimum strength, and the internal field is at maximum strength; sunspots appear on the photosphere. A solar minimum occurs when the polarity changes for the next 11-year cycle; the external field becomes maximum strength, and the internal field the minimum strength. The magnetic north and south poles are changed, and sunspots are relatively rare.

The solar magnetic field extends beyond the sun and leads to many effects that are collectively called solar activities. The effects of solar activities on earth include auroras at moderate to high latitudes and the disruptions of radio communications and electric power.

Solar activity has been thought to have played a role in the formation and evolution of the solar system.

Satellites surrounding the earth can be affected by the 11/22-year solar cycle and the related sun spots.

Long-term changes in sunspots correlated with solar radiation in the 17th century when very few sunspots were observed. It appeared that the solar cycle stopped for several decades during the "Little Ice Age" that extended from about 1350 to 1850 AD Europe experienced unusually cold temperatures.

Sun has behavioral changes at 41,000 year and 100,000 year cycles. It is possible that the 11/22-year cycle, the 41,000-year cycle and the 100,000 cycles may have an impact on earth's weather. On the other hand, there is no evidence that the sun has an impact on global warming.

GEOLOGIC EONS, ERAS AND PERIORDS

GEOLOGIC EONS, ERAS AND PERIODS

EON	ERA	ICE AGE	PERIODS	AGE
		Quaternary	Antropocene	2040 (?) A.D. -1950 A.D.
		Quaternary	Holocene	1950 A.D. - 12,000 B.C,
		Quaternary	Late pleistocene	12,000 B .C. -2.6 million years ago
Phanerozoic	Cenozoic	Late Cenozoic	Neogene	23-2.6 million years ago
Phanerozoic	Cenozoic	Late Cenozoic	Paleogene	66-23 million years ago
Phanerozoic	Mesozoic		Cretaceous	145-66 million years ago
Phanerozoic	Mesozoic		Jurassic	201-145 million years ago
Phanerozoic	Mesozoic		Triassic	252-201 million years ago
Phanerozoic	Paleozoic	Karoo	Permian	299-252 million years ago
Phanerozoic	Paleozoic	Karoo	Carboniferous	359-299 million years ago
Phanerozoic	Paleozoic		Devonian	419-359 million years ago
Phanerozoic	Paleozoic		Silurian	444-419 million years ago
Phanerozoic	Paleozoic	Ordovician	Ordovician	485-444 million years ago
Phanerozoic	Paleozoic		Cambrian	541-485 million years ago
Precambrian	Proterozoic	Snow Ball	Neoproterozoic	1000-541 million years ago
	Proterozoic		Mesoproterozoic	1600-1000 million years ago
	Proterozoic	Huron	Paleproterozoic	2500-1600 million years ago
	Archean		Neoarchean	2800-2500 million years ago
	Archean	Pondgola	Mesoarchean	3200-2800 million years ago
	Archean		Paleoarchean	3600-3200 million years ago
	Archean		Eoarchean	4000-3600 million years ago
	Hadean		Hadean	4600-4000 million years ago

SOURCES OF INFORMATION

(1)   Environmental matters   independent source environmental information

(2)   Global Warming 101   April 7, 2021,   Amanda MacMillan and Jeff Turrentine. Unidentified report on the internet.

(3)   Global warming   NASA Earth Observatory

(4)   Global warming   unidentified reports on the internet

(5)   Greenhouse gas   Wikipedia

(6)   How much solar energy is required   KubyEnergy.ca to power Alberta

(7)   Earth is warmed by Radiation   unidentified report on the internet

(8) CO_2 Ice Core Data   D.M. Etheridge, L.P. Steele, R.L. Lingfield's, RJ Francey, J.M. Barnola, and V.I. Morgan. 1998: Historical CO2 records from the Law Dome DE08, DE08-2, and DSS ice cores. In Trends: A Compendium of Data on global change. Carbon Dioxide Information Center, Oak Ridge National Laboratory, US Department of Energy, Oak Ridge, Tenn., USA.

(9)   66 million Years of Earth's Climate History Uncovered - Puts

(10)   Current changes in Context: September 10, 2020: University of California

(11)   Temperatures (2500 BC- 2040):   January   10, 2021: meteorologist Randy Mann,

(12)   Internet report.

(13)   500-year temperature change   Smithsonian National Museum

(14)   Earth's orbit and earth's axial tilt   Unidentified internet report

(15)   Photosynthesis   Wikipedia

(16)   How do greenhouse gases trap heat

(17)   in the atmosphere? Brittany Andrews, M.I.T. report

(18)   (18)   Wetland Wikipedia

(19)   Peat   Wikipedia

(20)   Volcanic gas   Wikipedia

(21)   Geology of the Canadian Rockies: Wikipedia, 5-page summary of a paper by Ben Gadd.

(22)   Magnetic Pole reversal happens   Internet: August 7, 2017, NASA content administrator all the (geologic) time:

(23)   Magnetic Reversal caused massive internet: Lauren Fuge, a Science journalist at Cosmos climate, shifts   Australia (?).
(24)   Earth's Orbit   Wikipedia
(25)   Milankovitch (Orbital) cycles and   Alan Buis, NASA's Jet Propulsion Laboratory Their role in earth's climate
(26)   The Earth's Changing Orbit Sue Ann Bowling
(27)   Methane Wikipedia
(28)   Natural gas   Wikipedia
(29)   Natural gas   Wikipedia
(30)   Natural gas in U.S.A.   Wikipedia
(31)   Natural gas in Canada   Wikipedia
(32)   Darvaza gas crater Wikipedia
(33)   Views from space reveal huge leaks   Morgan McFall-Johnsen, In the US and Asia. This could be easy
(34)   Spots to cut emissions and money
(35)   Satellite images show the biggest methane   Adam Vaughn; European Space Agency Leaks come from Russia and US.
(36)   Researchers shed new light on methane Jacob dick, LNG INSIGHT "Ultra-emitters" with satellite analysis
(37)   Seen from Space: Huge Methane Leaks Henry Fountain
(38)   What is Natural Gas   Fundamentals of Natural Gas, An International perspective, Penn Well Corporation, 2006.
(39)   Forest fires   Wikipedia
(40)   Forest fires   Wikipedia
(41)   Forest fires   Pacific Institute for Climate Solutions
(42)   Ecology Global Press
(43)   Do greenhouse gasses produce drought: Jessica Merzdorf Evans, NASA's Goddard space
(44)   flight Center.
(45)   Drought in the USA.   Jessica Merzdorf Evans, NASA's Goddard Space Flight Center
(46)   Drought Wikipedia
(47)   Palliser's Triangle Wikipedia
(48)   Carbon dioxide   Wikipedia
(49)   Carbon   Wikipedia
(50)   Graphite Wikipedia
(51)   Limestone   Wikipedia
(52)   Cement and Quick lime   Wikipedia
(53)   Ocean
(54)   History of Water on Earth   Wikipedia

(55)   How do Hurricanes form   Nasa Science
         (https://scienc.nasa.gov.)
(56)   Water cycle   Wikipedia
(57)   Flooding Wikipedia
(58)   Heavy Flooding and Global Internet, Published March 23, 2010
         Warming: Is there a connection?
(59)   The atmosphere of Earth   Wikipedia
(60)   Nitrogen Wikipedia
(61)   Oxygen   Wikipedia
(62)   Great oxidation Event   Wikipedia
(63)   timeline of Glaciation   Wikipedia
(64)   Major icc ages   Wikipedia
(65)   Little ice age   Wikipedia
(66)   Little ice age   unidentified report on the internet
(67)   Mid-Pleistocene Transition   Unidentified internet report
(68)   Permian - Triassic extinction event   Wikipedia
(69)   Dinosaurs   Wikipedia
(70)   Major Ice Ages   Wikipedia
(71)   Karoo Ice Age   Wikipedia
(72)   Late Ordovician Glaciation Wikipedia
(73)   Timeline of glaciation   Wikipedia
(74)   Sun   Wikipedia
(75)   David Zuzuki   C.B.C., Nature of Things, Wild Canadian
         Weather, May 28, 2022.
(76)   Rebecca Lindsey   Climate change: atmospheric carbon dioxide,
         June 23, 2022.
(77)   Kathryn Hansen   NASA, global climate change, October 17,
         2010
(78)   Pliocene Climate   Wikipedia, 2022

ABOUT THE AUTHOR

Dr. William Petruk is a retired Research Scientist in the field of Applied Mineralogy in earth sciences, especially in relationship to metallurgy. He was widely recognized for his work, both nationally and internationally, and was invited to conduct short courses and seminars at scientific institutes, universities, private research laboratories and United Nations courses in Europe, Australia, South America, and USA. Upon retirement, his hobby was studying scientific reports in mining and related fields, including global warming. This book summarizes and co-ordinates most of the current scientific research on global warming, and integrates it with his knowledge of earth sciences.